S.S.F. Public Library
West Orange
840 West Orange Ave.
South San Francisco, CA 94080

South San Francisco Public Library

3 9048

D0763016

The Girls' Guide to Growing Up

Choices & Changes in the Tween Years

Terri Couwenhoven, M.S.

Woodbine House ❀ 2011

© 2012 Terri Couwenhoven
First edition

All rights reserved. Published in the United States of America by Woodbine House, Inc., 6510 Bells Mill Road, Bethesda, MD 20817. 800-843-7323. www.woodbinehouse.com.

Illustrations on pages 3, 6, 7-10, 12-13, 16-19, 26, 39-42, 44-45, and 57 by Gary Mohrman.

Library of Congress Cataloging-in-Publication Data

Couwenhoven, Terri.
  The girls' guide to growing up : choices & changes in the tween years / by Terri Couwenhoven. -- 1st ed.
      p. cm.
  Includes index.
  ISBN 978-1-60613-026-1
  1. Teenage girls--Physiology--Juvenile literature. 2. Sex instruction for children with mental disabilities. 3. Puberty--Juvenile literature. I. Title.
  RJ144.C68 2011
  613'.04242--dc23

                                                  2011030826

Manufactured in the United States of America

10   9   8   7   6   5   4   3

This book is dedicated to
the girls and moms in my puberty
workshops who taught me that
understandable information
is a powerful thing.

Table of Contents

CARING FOR YOUR BODY

PUBLIC OR PRIVATE?

FINAL WORDS

Puberty Basics

What Is Puberty?

This book will help you get ready for an important time in your life. This time is called **puberty**.

Puberty is the time when kids begin to grow up. During puberty, your body will change in many ways. Some changes will make you **look** more like a woman. Other changes will make you **feel** more like a woman.

The changes that happen are normal and happen to everyone!

Both boys and girls go through puberty. But this book is just about changes that happen to girls.

Look at the picture of the girl and the woman on the next page. Can you see how their bodies are different?

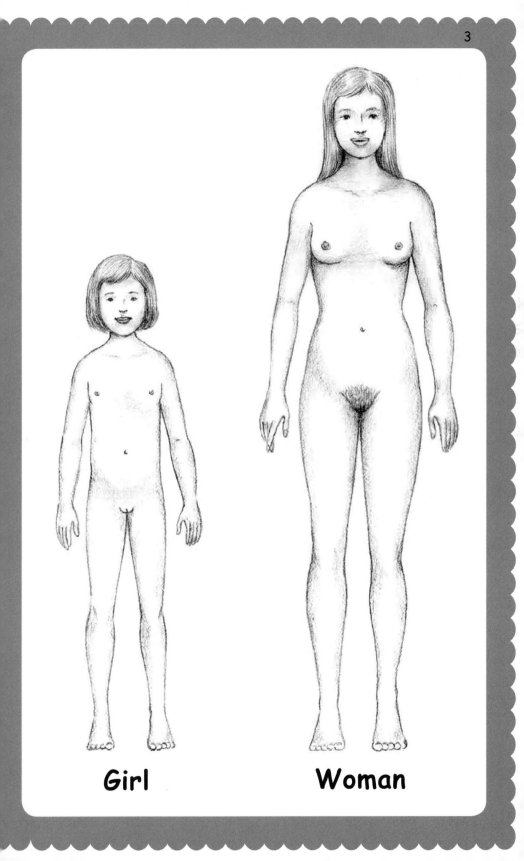

Girl   Woman

When Will You Begin Puberty?

The short answer is: between age 9 and 14. That's when most girls start puberty.

Here's the long answer:

Puberty will start when your body is ready. Your body might start to change at age 9 or 10. Or the changes might start a little later—at age 11 or 12. Some girls don't see any changes until age 13 or 14.

Your body will change at its own speed. It will take a few years before you look like a grown woman.

Let's talk about the ways your body will change during puberty.

Outside Changes

What Changes Will You See?

Body changes you can see are called outside changes. When you see these changes, it means you are starting puberty.

Changes in your. . . GROWTH

During puberty your body will grow in many ways!

* ❁ You will get taller and you will need larger clothes.

* ❁ Your feet will grow and you will need bigger shoes.

* ❁ Your hips will get rounder, curvier, and not so straight.

These body changes are normal. They happen to all girls during puberty.

It will take a few years for your body to stop growing and changing. When puberty is over, you will look like a woman.

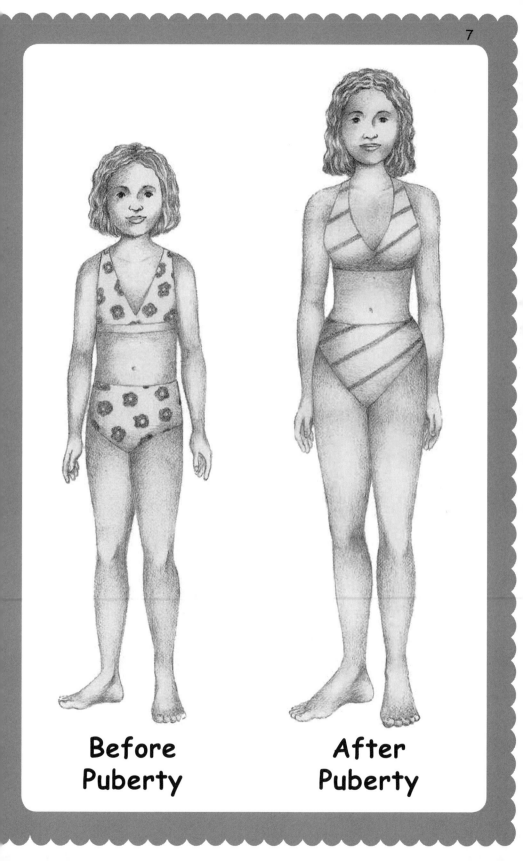

Before
Puberty

After
Puberty

Changes in Your . . .
BREASTS

During puberty, girls start to grow breasts (or boobs).

Everyone is different, so breasts can grow to be different sizes. Some girls grow smaller breasts. Other girls grow larger breasts.

It will take a few years for your breasts to stop growing. When puberty is done, your breasts will be the best size for you.

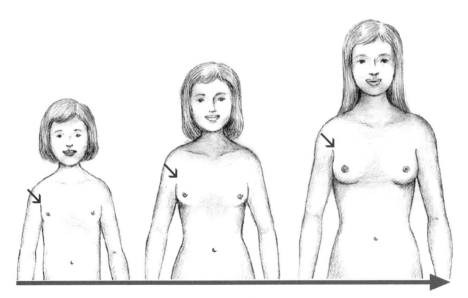

Breast Changes

All about Bras

When do you need to start wearing a **bra?** You will need one when your breasts start to grow. Older girls and women wear bras every day. A bra will help support your breasts. It will also make your clothes look nice.

Bras are sold in stores that sell underclothes. Your mom (or another adult woman) can take you to the store to try on different kinds.

Bras come in many styles and colors. Pick one that fits your personality and feels the best.

PRIVATE It's exciting to grow breasts and wear a bra. But it is **private.** Keep information about what is happening to your body—especially your private parts— to yourself. If you have questions, talk to your parent or another adult you trust.

Changes in your . . .
HAIR

During puberty, you will grow more hair. Hair will grow in new places on your body. It will grow in places where you never had hair before.

You will notice hair growing on the private area between your legs. This area is called the vulva. Hair that grows here is called pubic hair.

At first, pubic hair will be soft and straight. Later it will turn darker and get curly.

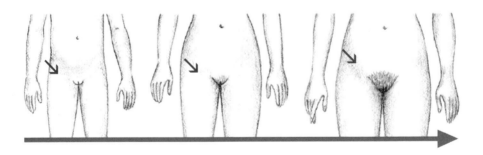

Hair will also grow under your arms. And hair on your legs will get darker and thicker.

Some teenaged girls shave the hair on their legs and under their arms—especially in summer or when they want to wear a swimsuit.

Shaving your legs and armpits takes practice. Your mom (or another adult woman) can teach you how to use a razor if you want to learn. Not all girls shave and that's normal too! You can decide if you want to shave.

PRIVATE Finding hair on new places of your body is normal but private. Keep information about what is happening to your body to yourself. If you have questions, talk to your parent or another adult you trust.

Changes in your . . . SKIN

During puberty, you might notice changes in your skin. Your face might get more oily or shiny. It might also get red bumps or sores called **pimples** (**zits** or **acne**). Some girls get pimples on their back, chest, or other body parts too.

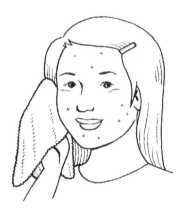

It's important to keep your skin clean. Be sure to wash your face in the morning when you get up and at night before bed. Try not to touch or squeeze pimples.

If the pimples hurt or won't go away, talk to your doctor.

What's That Smell?

Skin changes can make you smell different too! **Body odor** (or **B.O.**) gets stronger during puberty.

What can you do so you won't stink?

❀ Wash your armpits and private parts.

❀ Try showering more often.

❀ Use deodorant.

Most girls start to use **deodorant** during puberty. Deodorant stops you from sweating so much. It also helps you smell better.

There are many kinds of deodorant. Some rub on dry. Others rub on wet. They all smell different too. You can decide if you want to smell like fruit, a flower, or just your natural you!

If you smell bad, people won't want to be near you. To stop odors, wash your body and use deodorant **every day**.

Inside Changes

What Changes Will You Feel?

Changes won't just happen outside of your body. There will be lots of inside changes too. You can't see these changes. But you might start to feel different.

Let's talk about changes happening inside your body during puberty.

Changes in Your . . . FEELINGS

During puberty, your feelings or moods can change a lot. One minute you may feel happy. The next minute, you may feel angry or sad. This is called being **moody**.

Feeling moody is normal. It happens to all girls during puberty. What causes these mood changes? Hormones!

Everyone's body makes hormones. Hormones send messages to your body to help it know what to do—like grow taller or go to sleep.

In puberty, you make new hormones. These hormones cause a lot of the body changes we talk about in this book. You can feel moody when these hormones move through your body.

Handling Your Moods

Part of growing up is learning how to handle your feelings. When you feel moody, here are some things you can do:

❀ Spend time doing fun things. Listen to music or watch a favorite TV show. What do you like to do to have fun?

❀ Move your body! Dancing, walking, or playing sports can help you feel better when you are having a bad day.

❀ Take time to be by yourself. Having private time away from other people can help.

❀ Write about your feelings or share your feelings with someone you trust.

Changes in . . .
SEXUAL FEELINGS

During puberty, you might have new and exciting feelings when you see or think about someone you like. This is called **having sexual feelings** or **having a crush**.

Some girls have crushes on TV and movie stars. Other girls have crushes on people at school or in the community. Some girls don't have these feelings at all. That's normal too!

PRIVATE Having crushes is **normal**. But these feelings are private. If you are in public and others are around, it is best to keep sexual feelings to yourself. It is OK to talk about these feelings with parents or other adults you trust. But be sure to talk in private!

Handling Crushes

Have you ever seen kids act differently when they are around someone they like? Maybe they use words to get a person to notice them. For example, they send love notes. Or they say "You're hot" or "I think you're cute." Or maybe

they use their bodies to get attention. They move closer to someone, smile, blink their eyes, or use a playful voice. This is called **flirting**.

Some kids (and adults) flirt with people they have crushes on. Flirting can help you find out if the other person likes you too. Flirting can be fun. But there are rules you should know:

* ❊ Only flirt with people who are about your same age.

* ❊ Do not flirt with adults (teachers, aides, store clerks, bus drivers, waiters or waitresses).

* ❊ Do not flirt when you need to be working or learning.

* ❊ Flirting can bother people if they don't feel the same way you do. If they are not interested, they might walk away or not flirt back. If someone does not seem interested in you, STOP!

When you are old enough to go on dates, you can talk about sexual feelings with the person you are dating. It is normal for people who are dating to share their feelings in private. They can say private things like: "You are beautiful" or "You are so much fun to be with" or "I like you a lot."

What ELSE Can You Do about Sexual Feelings?

Some girls touch their private body parts when they are alone. They do this when they have sexual feelings or think about someone they like. This can feel good.

Touching or rubbing your private body parts is called **masturbation**. Some girls do not like to touch their private parts. That is normal too. (See page 44 if you are not sure which body parts are private.)

PRIVATE Touching your vulva, breasts, or butt is very **private**. (That's why they are called private parts!) Make sure you are in your bedroom by yourself with the door closed.

Periods

What's a Period?

Now we come to one of the most important changes. This change is also one of the biggest! It is called **menstruation** or **getting a period.**

You know that dot at the end of a sentence? That's one kind of period. But this is different.

Getting your period means that blood from inside your body will come out of an opening between your legs. This opening is called the **vagina.**

When you get a period, blood will come out of your vagina for four or five days. Then it will stop. But the next month, you will get another period. Once your periods start, you will have one every month.

June

Mo	Tu	We	Th	Fr	Sa	Su
			1	2	3	4
5	6	7	8	9	10	11
12	13	14	15	16	17	18
19	20	21	22	23	24	25
26	27	28	29	30		

July

Mo	Tu	We	Th	Fr	Sa	Su
					1	2
3	4	5	6	7	8	9
10	11	12	13	14	15	16
17	18	19	20	21	22	23
24 31	25	26	27	28	29	30

Periods Are Normal!

Really? It is normal for blood to come out of your body?!

Yes. When you see blood during your period, it does not mean you are hurt. And nothing is wrong. Having a period is a sign that your body is healthy, normal, and working like it should.

Remember, your body is growing and changing during puberty. Getting a period is one of the inside changes.

The picture on page 26 shows the inside body parts that change during puberty. It shows where the blood comes from and where it comes out.

Periods Are Private!

Most girls have lots of questions about periods. Getting a period is a huge change! You can find answers to some questions girls often have on pages 51 to 57.

PRIVATE

Getting a period is normal. It happens to all girls. But having a period is private. Keep information about your period to yourself. If you have questions, talk to your parent or another adult you trust.

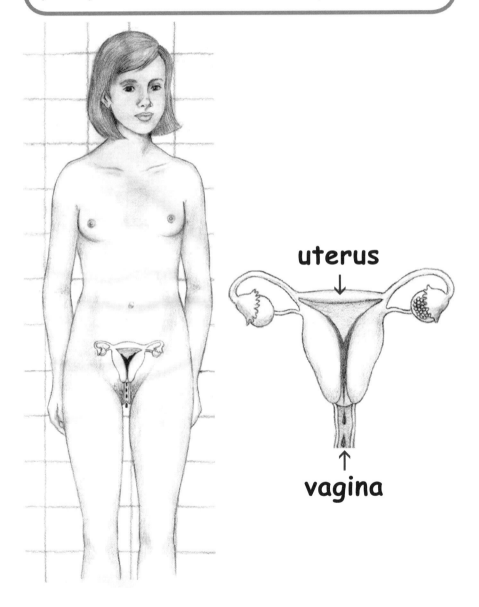

uterus
↓

↑
vagina

Handling Your Period

You will need to wear a **pad** every day when you are having a period. Wearing pads keeps the blood from getting on your clothes.

You and your mom can buy pads at grocery stores or drug stores. There are many kinds of pads. Some are thick and some are thin. Some are long and some are shorter. Some are for wearing during the day, and others at night. Some even have "wings" that wrap around the sides of your underwear. (But these wings will not help you fly!)

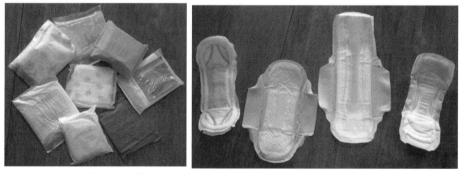

Some pads in their wrappers

Some pads unwrapped

You will need to find a pad that feels comfortable and doesn't leak. Try out different kinds and see what works best for you!

How Do You Use a Pad?

Learning how to use a pad when you have a period is part of growing up. Here are some pictures that can help you learn how.

Step 1: When you see blood in your underwear, get a pad.

You see blood in your underwear.

Get a pad.

PRIVATE Putting on a pad is private, so pads are kept in private places like the bathroom. Have your mom show you where pads are kept in your house.

At school, you can keep pads in your locker, purse, or backpack. If you notice blood in your underwear at school, tell your teacher or the nurse in private. They can help you find a pad if you need one.

Step 2: Take the pad to the bathroom. Changing a pad is private.

Take the pad to the bathroom.

Shut the door.

Take pad out.

Step 3: Open the pad. Stick it in the crotch of your underwear.

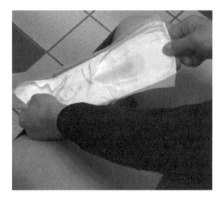

Unwrap the pad.

Throw out the wrapper.

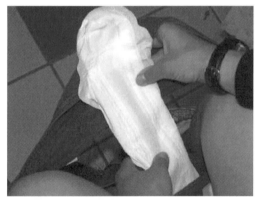

Stick the pad in your underwear.

Make sure pad won't fall out and is in the right place.

Step 4: Dress and clean up.

Pull up your underwear.

Pull up your pants.

Wash your hands.

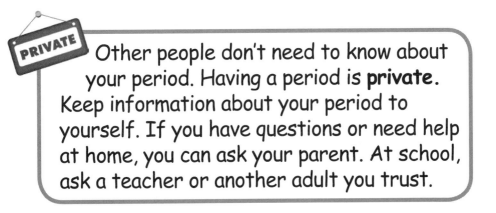

PRIVATE

Other people don't need to know about your period. Having a period is **private**. Keep information about your period to yourself. If you have questions or need help at home, you can ask your parent. At school, ask a teacher or another adult you trust.

How Do You Know when to Change Your Pad?

When you are having your period, you must change your pad often. If you don't, blood will get on your clothes.

Most girls need to put on a new pad after 2 or 3 hours. At school, that might be after 2 or 3 classes. At home, that might be after a video or a couple TV shows.

If you are not sure if you should change your pad, just do it! If you wait too long, blood might get on your clothes. Then other people will know you are having your period. That can be embarrassing!

PRIVATE
Other people do not need to know you are changing your pad. It is private. You can talk to your parent, a teacher, or another adult woman if you have questions or need help.

Which Pad Needs to Be Changed?

Look at these photos. Point to the pad you think should be changed now.

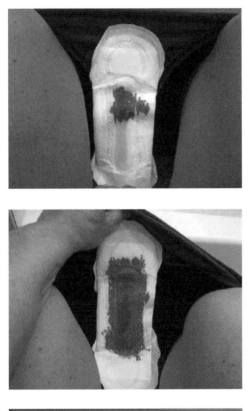

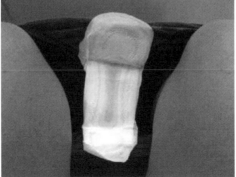

Caring for Your Body

Keeping Your Body Clean

Once you begin puberty, it means you are growing up! This is a good time to start practicing to be an adult. Part of being an adult is keeping your body clean. Keeping your body clean and smelling fresh is called having **good hygiene.**

Look at the list below. Try to match the body change (on the left) with the action you need to take for good hygiene (on the right):

When you notice:	You will need to:
Breasts growing	Find a pad
Oily skin or pimples	Shower and use deodorant
Blood on your clothes	Wash your face
Your pad is full of blood	Wash your hair (or take a shower)
Greasy hair	Buy a bra and wear it every day
Body odor	Change your pad

Keeping Yourself Safe

You are growing up and learning to be an adult now. Part of being an adult is learning rules about your body. These rules will help you be safe at home and in public.

Rules for Your Body and Private Body Parts

Now that your body is changing into a woman's body, you need to be **modest**. This means keep your private body parts covered when others are around. If you are not sure which body parts are private, look at page 44.

Here are some rules:
* Keep your clothes on when you are in public.

* Wear a robe if you have to walk from the bathroom to your bedroom after bathing.

* Close your bedroom door when you are changing clothes.

- In a locker room, don't stare at other girls' bodies. Always keep your hands to yourself.

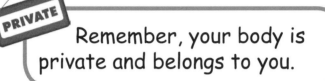

Remember, your body is private and belongs to you.

Touching Rules for Your Own Body

You get to decide when and if you want to be touched.

If someone touches you and you don't want to be touched, you can shout:

- "NO!"
- "STOP!" or
- "I DON'T LIKE THAT!"

STOP!

NO!

I DON'T LIKE THAT!

Or, you can use your body to let someone know you don't want to be touched. You can:

❀ Put your hand up to say "stop."

❀ Shake your head "no."

❀ Walk away.

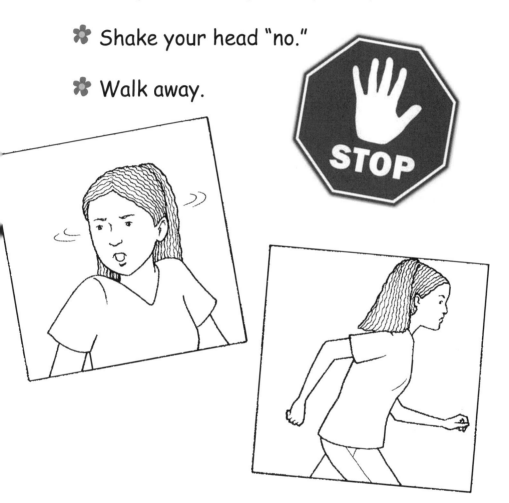

IMPORTANT: There are a few times (only two) when people may need to touch you even if you don't want to be touched. This might happen if your body or private parts need care. Can you think of examples?

People Who Can Touch or Look at Your Body

1. **Your doctor or a nurse.**
Keeping your body **healthy** is part of growing up. Your doctor or nurse might need to look at you when you are undressed. He or she might need to touch or check your private parts. A doctor's job is to check your body to make sure it is healthy. This includes your private parts.

2. **Your mother or another adult helper.**
Keeping your body clean is part of growing up. Some girls need help learning how to clean their bodies. While you are learning, it is OK for your mother or another safe person to help you clean yourself. Your parents will tell you who can help you with hygiene if you need help.

REMEMBER: Only your doctor, nurse, mother, or adult helper can look at or touch your private parts. It is not OK for anybody else to see or touch them.

If this happens, you should:

Say "No!"

Get away.

Tell an adult who will listen.

Rules for Touching Others

Nobody is allowed to touch you without your permission, right? Well . . . guess what? You should not touch other people unless they say it is OK. It is best to ask before touching people you know.

Not everybody likes to be touched. Sometimes people you are trying to hug might say no or walk away. That means they don't want to be touched.

If you are meeting someone for the first time, you can shake hands and say, "Nice to meet you." This is how adults touch if they are meeting someone new.

It is not OK to touch or hug people you do not know. It is never OK to touch or look at another person's private body parts. If someone asks you to look at or touch their private body parts, you should:

Say "No!"	Get away.	Tell an adult.

What Are the Private Body Parts?

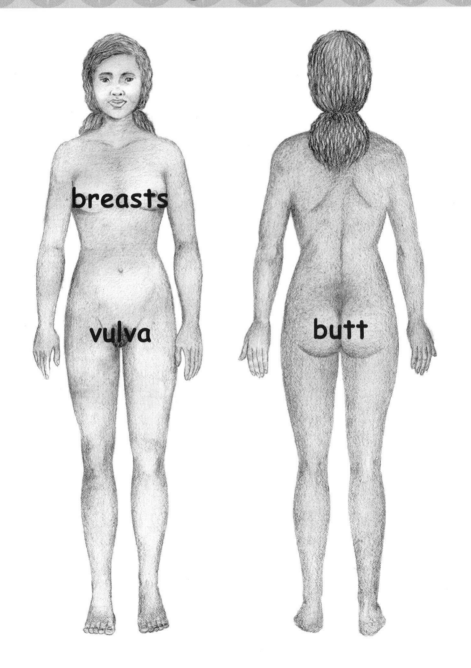

breasts

vulva

butt

Public or Private?

Once puberty is over, you will look like an adult (not a little girl). When you look like an adult, people you meet will want you to act like a grown-up. So, you need to learn grown-up rules for what you can say and do in public and private.

Let's review what these two words mean:

PUBLIC means that other people are around. Can you think of one of your favorite public places?

public

PRIVATE means that you are alone. Nobody can see or hear you. Do you have a private place at home? What is it?

private

Public and Private Quiz

Here is a list of things that girls do. Seven of them should only be done in private. Do you know which ones?

DIRECTIONS:
Circle the **bold** letter in each sentence that talks about something private.

Then write the letters down, in order, on a piece of paper. Do the letters spell a word?

1. Change your **P**ad.

2. **A**sk where the restroom is.

3. Eat an **I**ce cream cone.

4. **R**ub deodorant under your arms.

5. Watch a **M**ovie with kissing in it.

6. Share **I**nformation about changes happening to your body.

7. **B**uy pads at the grocery store.

8. Touch your **V**ulva.

9. **A**sk questions about getting a period or wearing a bra.

10. Wear a bikini at the **P**ool.

11. **T**ake a shower.

12. Tell a knock-knock **J**oke.

13. Tell your teacher you don't have **E**nough pads.

Answer (Turn upside-down!)

The private things are in sentences 1, 4, 6, 8, 9, 11, 13. They spell the word **private**.

Final
Words

Growing Up Is Normal!

It is exciting to change from a girl to a woman. But it can also be a little scary. It is normal to have questions about what is going on!

When you have questions, talk to a parent or another adult you trust. Other people don't need to know what is happening to your body. Remember, body changes are private.

Puberty is normal and happens to all girls. It's part of growing up!

Common Questions and Answers about Periods

Do boys and men get periods?
No! Only puberty-aged girls and adult women have periods.

Is it scary when the blood comes out?
Your first period can be a little scary because you don't know when it will come. And it is something new and different for you.

This book was made to help you learn all about periods and how normal they are. When you know what is happening and what to expect, you won't be afraid.

Remember that all girls have periods. It is a sign that your body is healthy and working like it should.

Can I stop the blood from coming out?
You cannot stop (or start) the blood from coming out of your vagina when you have your period. The blood comes from inside

of your uterus. (See the picture on page 26.) The uterus is not a muscle that you can squeeze (like when you stop yourself from peeing).

When your period starts, you have to use a pad until the bleeding stops and your period is done.

Will I ever stop having periods?

Yes! Periods **start** coming during puberty. Later, when you are much older, they will **stop.**

Periods stop when women are in their 40s or 50s. The word for this is **menopause.** When a woman has gone through menopause, it means she does not get periods any more.

Do I need to wear a pad at night while I sleep?

Yes! The blood comes out of your vagina even when you are sleeping. So, you need to wear underwear with a pad under your pajamas.

Some girls and women need to use special nighttime pads. These pads soak up more blood so you can sleep through the night. You do not have to wake up and change your pad.

How can I tell what day my period will start?

There is no way to know what day you will get your first period. But your body will give you clues. Are you growing breasts? Do you have pubic hair? Do you feel moody? These are signs that your period might start soon!

After you have had a few periods, they will start coming around the same date every month. To help you know when it is time to get your period, try this:

On a calendar, circle the date you started your period. For example, it started on June 4. So, circle June 4. Then circle the same date of the next month. For example, circle July 4.

June						
Mo	Tu	We	Th	Fr	Sa	Su
			1	2	3	4
5	6	7	8	9	10	11
12	13	14	15	16	17	18
19	20	21	22	23	24	25
26	27	28	29	30		

July						
Mo	Tu	We	Th	Fr	Sa	Su
					1	2
3	4	5	6	7	8	9
10	11	12	13	14	15	16
17	18	19	20	21	22	23
24 31	25	26	27	28	29	30

Your period might not come exactly on the date that you circled. But it will probably come a few days before or a few days after. Keeping track can help you plan ahead. That way you can be ready.

What if I am not at home when my period starts?

There is no way to tell when your first period will come. So, plan ahead! You and your mom can make a plan so you will know what to do. Here are some ideas:

❁ Keep a few pads in your backpack or purse. That way you will have a pad with you if you notice blood in your underwear.

❁ You and your mom can put a few pads in a private place in the car. This will help if you are away from home when your period comes.

❁ If you are at someone else's house and need a pad, talk to another adult woman. All women have periods, so they will understand. They should be able to help you find a pad.

What should I do if blood gets on my clothes?

This happens to all girls (and even adult women). If you get blood on your clothes at home, change into clean clothes. Then put on a pad. Put the clothes with blood on them in a tub or sink. Cover them with **cold** water until they can be washed.

Bring extra clothes to leave at school in case this happens at school. If you get blood on your clothes at school, change into your extra clothes. Then bring the dirty clothes home to soak and wash later. If you need help, ask a woman teacher in private for help.

Can I take a shower or bath when I'm having a period?

Yes! It is very important to keep your body clean during your period. When you take a bath or shower, your period will slow down or stop while you are bathing. After you leave the shower or bath, you will begin bleeding again. So, make sure you have underwear and a clean pad ready.

Can I go swimming when I have my period?

Girls who use pads cannot go into a pool or lake when they have their period. If the pad gets wet, it will rip apart and pieces will stay in the water. This is not healthy.

If you want to swim during your period, you need to learn how to use a **tampon.** A tampon is another way to catch the blood that comes out of the vagina during your period. It is harder to learn how to use a tampon. It takes lots of practice. That's because tampons go inside the vagina and can't be seen.

If you want to try using a tampon instead of a pad, talk to your mom or another adult woman so they can help.

Why do girls and women have periods?

Getting periods is the way your body practices for growing a baby. Each month, the uterus grows a layer of blood and tissue just in case a baby is growing.

Of course, most of the time there is no baby in the uterus. So, that layer of blood and tissue is not needed. If there is no baby in the uterus, the blood and tissue comes out of the vagina and the woman gets her period. (See page 26.)

There is only one way a baby can grow inside the uterus. That is if a sperm from the man and an egg from the woman join together. This can **only** happen when a man and a woman have sex. Grown-up couples decide to have a baby when they feel they can handle all the work of taking care of another person.

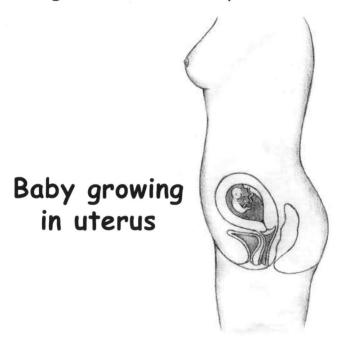

Baby growing in uterus

Women (and girls) still get their periods each month even if they decide that they never want to have a baby!

Index

About the Author

Terri Couwenhoven, M.S., is an AASECT certified sexuality educator who specializes in working with people who have intellectual disabilities, their families, and the professionals who support them.

She is the author of **Teaching Children with Down Syndrome about Their Bodies, Boundaries, and Sexuality: A Guide for Parents and Professionals** and other publications. When she is not teaching, she is Clinic Coordinator for the Down Syndrome Clinic at Children's Hospital of Wisconsin.

Terri has two daughters; her oldest has Down syndrome.